Forgiveness

Walk Me Through It

Forgiveness

Walk Me Through It

All scripture taken from the New King James Version.
Copyright © 1979, 1980, 1982 by Thomas Nelson, Inc. Used by permission. All rights reserved.

Second Revision

© Copyright 2010 Charlie Holley All Rights Reserved

Dedications

To my beautiful wife Cassandra. I know your constant struggle with forgiveness. And I also know what God has spoken over your life. I know He will show you the way and fulfill His promises to you. May you find His joy in forgiveness through this book.

To my spiritual son Orlando. Your life has been extremely difficult, but God will give you double for your troubles. I pray you will use this book to find the forgiveness you've longed for.

To my spiritual daughter Carmen. You have endured many "wounds" throughout your life and yet you still manage to stand in the power of God. May this book take you into completing the forgiveness you've already started.

To my spiritual father Pastor O.W. Davis. I've watched you from afar and learned many valuable spiritual lessons. You've had much in your life to forgive, and still you rise to complete what God has for you. May you find a peace in this book that surpasses all understanding.

To all those whose life is a constant uphill struggle and a consistent battle to find the happiness that once was. May God heal your wounds and restore the good things in your life.

Table of Contents

Introduction: Lord help me through this. 9

Chapter One: Forgiveness: A working definition 15

Chapter Two: Misconceptions of Forgiveness 21

Chapter Three: Forgiveness: Why is it so hard? 29

Chapter Four: Developing the Proper Motivation 35

Chapter Five: Help Me Desire It: Taking a closer look. 41

Chapter Six: Forgiveness from the heart 49

Chapter Seven: Walk Me Through It: God's Justice 55

Chapter Eight: Dealing With the Anger 61

Chapter Nine: Receiving God's Peace 67

Chapter Ten: Learning to Trust God 71

Chapter Eleven: How do I forgive Myself? 75

Chapter Twelve: The Healing Starts With You! 79

Chapter Thirteen: Forgiveness – The Need for God. 85

Chapter Fourteen: It's Not About You! 89

Forgiveness Journal 93

Introduction

Lord, Help Me Through This!

~Stories of Struggles~

I've often held the opinion that forgiveness is the most difficult act of Christianity. I don't think I'm alone in this line of thinking. As you read the following fiction accounts in this introduction and throughout the book, try to identify points in their stories that are similar to the ones you may be experiencing.

Jake's stomach twisted in knots as he sat in the courtroom listening to testimony about the murder. As his swollen and tear-soaked eyes moved slowly toward the accused murderer, he could envision the accused strapped in an electric chair with his own hands firmly on the power switch.

It was difficult for Jake to imagine how someone could take the life of his twelve-year-old daughter in such a cold and callous manner. He wanted with all his heart to take matters into his own hands. Instead, he momentarily pushed aside the anger, buried his face in his hands, and wept bitterly.

Jeneva rang the doorbell to her father's house, but she didn't want to. As she stood on the porch nervously waiting for the elderly man to answer the door, her mind faded back to those moments of abuse and neglect he inflicted on her as a child.

Those wounds of abuse had managed to destroy her twelve-year marriage and separate her from her children. Now, two years after a divorce and release from a mental institution, Jeneva was finally preparing to confront the man whom she often said, "Destroyed my life."

When the phone rang, Rhonda peered at the caller-ID screen and refused to answer. As the rings continued, the name displayed on the ID inflamed her. It had been four years now since the divorce was final, but the physical and emotional wounds from her ex-husband's actions were still fresh.

She thought, "I gave him twenty-seven years of my life! How could he treat me like this?" When the rings persisted, she snatched the phone from the cradle and yelled into it, "What do you want!"

Alvin stared into the television set but wasn't interested in the show. His wife, noticing his far-away appearance, asked, "Alvin, honey what's wrong?"

Alvin muffled, "Nothing. It's nothing." He didn't want to go into it at the moment. In fact, he managed to avoid the subject for their entire marriage.

He didn't want his wife to know about his dead-beat dad who left his mother and three siblings to struggle for themselves while he had the time of his life. They heard from him once in a blue moon, but all Alvin had for him was contempt and hatred. He longed to experience the relationship of a true father.

Jodie tried with all she had to fit in with the discussion group, but something within her wouldn't allow it. She thought, "I don't belong here. All of these people are filled with so much anger and bitterness. Is this a picture of me in the upcoming years?"

"Group, we have a new member tonight and her name is Jodie." The counselor for the rape recovery group announced. "Jodie, would you like to share some thoughts with the group?"

Jodie thought for a moment. It surprised her that the first thoughts she wanted to share were those of anger and hatred

Forgiveness

for her convicted rapist. As she began to speak, tears welled up in her eyes and a knot formed in her stomach. She hung her head and motioned to the counselor to continue with the discussion without her.

It was extremely noisy in the day care center. As Trina sat in the lobby, waiting for the instructor to bring her three year-old daughter, suddenly another anxiety attack struck. It hadn't happened in quite some time, but suddenly she heard the cries of infant babies ringing in her ears. Her hands began to sweat as she sprang to her feet, covered her mouth with her hands, and ran out of the center into the fresh air.

As she stood close to the road, gasping for air, the thoughts of the horror of four years ago returned. Trina had forgiven her boyfriend for persuading her to have an abortion, but the person she found the most difficult to forgive was herself.

Can you find yourself somewhere in these stories? These are pictures of people attempting to live their lives in unforgiveness. Granted, they all have a right to be angry and bitter. People and situations in their lives had disappointed them and they ended up severely hurt.

While it is true that their lives will never be the same, it is also true that their lives aren't over. Their joy hadn't left for good and their happiness hadn't disappeared, that is, if they could find it in their hearts to forgive.

Perhaps they, like so many others, thought forgiveness is a license to free those who wronged them. They needed to be told that forgiveness is not a get-out-of-jail-free card. It's a promise to release their own lives from the bondage of anger and bitterness.

They also needed to know that unforgiveness does nothing to those who hurt them. It only allows confinement of themselves to a jail cell of the mind and holds them hostage to an emotional roller coaster. The only way out is found in the key called forgiveness.

In this book, we will explore some misconceptions, the true meaning of forgiveness, reasons we should forgive, and take a walk through forgiveness. We will complete the various stories and use them as examples to demonstrate forgiveness. We pray this book will release your soul and restore peace and happiness in your life. We invite you to step into these pages and be forever changed!

Chapter One Preview

Forgiveness: A Working Definition

A look at what's ahead:

- The two phases of forgiveness
- Speaking forgiveness from the heart
- Working out forgiveness in our lives
- The disciplines of forgiveness

Chapter 1

Forgiveness: A Working Definition

There are many definitions of forgiveness emanating from the world and even from the Christian community. This book is not written with the intent of developing a theological definition of forgiveness. However, for the sake of being of one mind with the reader, we will share this working definition of forgiveness.

Forgiveness is an act of obedience to God's will that leads us into peace and freedom from anger, hatred, and guilt. Forgiveness can be broken down into two phases. The first phase is instant but the second phase could last for years.

Phase I: Speaking the words of forgiveness from our heart.

Speaking forgiveness from the heart can be put in these terms: Speaking with the intent to carry out what was spoken regardless of how we feel.

It has nothing to do with emotions, but everything to do with our intentions. When we speak from the heart, we have every intention of demonstrating forgiveness in our lifestyle. That means we make a commitment to follow the discipline of forgiveness as we rely on the power of the Holy Spirit to see it to completion.

At times when our spirit is whispering "forgive", but our mind is yelling "never", it's the guiding of the Holy Spirit that gives us the strength and grace to do what is right. For without Him, we can do nothing that is good and pleasing in the eyes of God.

Our Lord and Savior provided us with the best example of phase-I forgiveness. While nailed to a roman cross and being humiliated by religious leaders, He spoke these words of forgiveness,

"Father, forgive them, for they do not know what they are doing."(Luke 23:34)

His words, spoken from the heart, reached the ears of the heavenly Father. And in doing so, He was following His own teachings and setting the example for generations to come. Just a few years later, a Holy Spirit filled disciple named Stephen would follow this example, and speak forgiveness while being stoned to death at the hands of those same religious leaders,

"Lord, do not charge them with this sin."(Acts 7:60)

God's Word instructs us to be men and women of our word. When we speak a certain thing, God expects us to live out the words. He says this,

"Death and life are in the power of the tongue... " (Proverbs 18:21)

"But let your 'yes' be 'yes', and your 'no,' 'no.'....." (Matthew 5:37)

Therefore, when we speak from the heart, we are obligating ourselves to demonstrate forgiveness. Fortunately, we don't have to do it alone. God provides His Holy Spirit, His Word, and the Blood of the Lamb to help us. God issues the grace and wisdom we need to carry out His pure instructions.

This is why we really cannot say, "I can't forgive because….." Even though forgiving is our choice, we are not expected to accomplish it through our power. It's not by our power or might, but by His Spirit!

Phase II: Working out the forgiveness that was spoken.

Working out forgiveness simply means living our lives in a manner that reflects forgiveness toward others. It involves something that is painful, time consuming, and challenging. We can sum this up in one word: **CHANGE!**

We must change the way we think, the things we do, the things we desire, and the things we know in order to gain the knowledge and wisdom of God. Here are a few things phase-II of forgiveness includes:

A. Constant prayer for the grace and strength of the Holy Spirit.

We are going to need the grace and strength of God in order to consistently carry out the disciplines of forgiveness.

B. Putting into practice certain disciplines.

- Not speaking ill of the person, especially in the presence of others.
- Not intentionally separating myself from them. However, there are times when separation is necessary (i.e. physical abuse or other serious dangers.)
- Refusing to seek vengeance, physically or emotionally.
- Helping the person when I have opportunity to do so.

C. Asking God for wisdom to change our point of view toward that person.

As we mature in our thinking and begin to see things from God's point of view, we will begin to welcome change and continue to become conformed into the image of Jesus Christ. Remember, His ways and thoughts are higher than ours (Isaiah 55:8-9).

Phase-II is a long drawn-out process, filled with successes and failures. How do we know when we are nearing the end of phase-II?

- When we are consistently practicing the disciplines mentioned above.
- When our desires begin to line up with those of God. (restoration)
- And when we no longer desire them to be "broken into bits and pieces", but that God would save and transform them into His likeness.

Now, we are truly being taken from "glory to glory" and reflecting like the water, the goodness and love of God to our enemy and the world!

Chapter Two Preview

Misconceptions of Forgiveness

A look at what's ahead:

- Forgiveness is not about our feelings.
- Forgiveness doesn't let others off.
- We should forgive quickly not slowly.
- We don't have to forget to forgive.

Chapter 2

Misconceptions of Forgiveness

We must come into the knowledge and understanding of what forgiveness means and involves. There are a variety of misconceptions about forgiveness. As a result, many have remained in an era of anger and pain. Divorces have taken place, family relationships have dissolved, and many have died in a bitter condition. Let's examine and correct a few of the widely accepted misconceptions. Here are some of the most common ones:

Misconception #1:

I Must Wait Until I No Longer Feel Angry Before Forgiving.

Forgiveness is not emotional (something we do based on our how we feel). We may tend to wait until all anger and ill feelings have somehow disappeared before we consider forgiving. It's a spiritual act that we voluntarily engage in. In other words, It's based on what the Word of God says. And according to His Word, we must forgive the wrongs committed against us,

"For if you forgive men their trespasses, your heavenly Father will also forgive you. But if you do not forgive men

their trespasses, neither will your heavenly Father forgive your trespasses." (Matthew 6:14-15)

Many have waited for the pain to disappear and for the anger to subside before considering forgiving. During this waiting period, we are taking a chance on loosing our lives and dying in unforgiveness. The pain and anger cannot be dealt with until forgiveness is first addressed. Now we may ask, "How do I forgive the way God wants me to?"

Jesus, the ultimate example, demonstrates this. They beat Him, spat on Him, and put a crown of thorns on His head. They marched Him up a rugged hill, and hung Him in the blistering sun, nailed to a wooden cross. Yet, before dying, He spoke these words,

"Father, forgive them, for they do not know what they are doing." Luke 23:34

We can confidently say Jesus was not in what some would call, "A forgiving mood". Jesus knew what God wanted of Him and He did what He had taught His disciples numerous times to do: to love and pray for those who misused them. Now, Jesus would set the example while on the cross. He spoke the words not from His emotions, but from His heart (according to the will of God).

We can conclude that forgiveness is not emotional; it's Spiritual. Therefore, we need not wait on the emotions of anger and hatred to disappear before doing what God expects of us. When we speak the words of forgiveness, regardless of how we feel, we are performing a spiritual act that God expects of us.

Misconception #2:

Forgiving Means Those Who Hurt Me Won't Be Punished.

In some ways, we may view our forgiveness as a "get out of jail free" card for those who have hurt us. In this situation we must understand what God calls "sowing and reaping." The word speaks in Galatians 6:7,

"Do not be deceived, God is not mocked; for whatever a man sows, that he will also reap." (Galatians 6:7)

This simply means that bad is punished and good is rewarded. Those who hurt us will be punished whether we forgive them or not. God will convict them by causing them to be aware of the terrible hurt they have brought upon us. Only God can convict. We cannot. When left up to us, all we can do is condemn.

When God begins to convict someone, we may not see the conviction in progress. In fact, they may try to convince the world and us that conviction isn't taking place. This often frustrates us because we want to see instantaneous results.

We must remember God's conviction is often a silent conviction. We cannot see what is taking place in a person's inner life, but we can be sure that God is at work on our behalf. We can be sure they are being shown the results of their actions and the hurt they have caused us.

Rest assured, our forgiveness doesn't grant a get out of jail free card to those who have hurt us. God will perform conviction, which in itself can be worse than the punishment. The nightmares, the heavy guilt, the sleepless nights, and the depression from a sin sick soul, can all take their toll, and in the end, become worse that the punishment itself.

Misconception #3:

I Can Forgive When I'm Ready. There is No Time Limit.

One of the most dangerous parts to play is that of a casual forgiver. At times, we can look for time limits and time frames for forgiveness. We tend to be like Peter who asks Jesus,

> "Lord, how often shall my brother sin against me, and I forgive him? Up to seven times?" (Matthew 18:21)

Often, we may think our unforgiveness is hurting those who hurt us. But we are the ones being hurt the most. The longer we live with unforgiveness in our hearts, the longer our relationships will suffer. Also, the longer we remain in unforgiveness, the longer we postpone our healing. One of the most difficult commands to carry out is,

> "Do not be overcome by evil, but overcome evil with good." (Romans 12:21)

In fact, at times, it can seem down right impossible! How can God expect me to do something good for someone who has caused me so much pain? What makes it even worse, is to see them live their lives as if they've done nothing wrong!

Like the author of Psalm 73, sometimes we can witness total injustice. The wicked seem to get off scott-free, and we are left to struggle with the broken pieces of our lives. The author says,

> "Behold, these are the ungodly, who are always at ease; they increase in riches." (Psalm 73:12)

We may witness them continue to perform evil, hurt others, and show no signs of repentance. However, the author eventually understands their fate:

> "Oh how they are brought to desolation, as in a moment! They are utterly consumed with terrors." (Psalm 73:19)

The author of the Psalm understood the end for those who do wrong. This understanding gave him comfort and helped him to see things from a better perspective. He knew the wicked weren't getting away; they were just temporarily getting by.

There weren't many things Jesus instructed us to do quickly, but forgiving was one of them. He speaks,

"Settle things with your adversary quickly, do it while you are on the way." (Matthew 5:25)

In conclusion, God doesn't want us to take our time forgiving! He wants us to do it quickly!

Misconception #4:

I Must Forget If I Truly Forgive.

We are blessed with something wonderful called remembrance. Our minds have the ability to recall the incidents of the past. Unfortunately, at least for some, our minds can recall the bad as well as the good.

Wouldn't it be wonderful if we could somehow program our minds to remember only the good? We would be able to conveniently forget all the heartaches and pains of the past and dwell on the good moments only.

Well, it's a nice thought, but no one has been able to pull it off. Try as we might, we cannot forget the horrible things that happened in our lives. This leaves some to feel as if they have not forgiven, simply because they can remember the incident. Our recollection need not be wiped out before we accomplish forgiveness.

True Forgiveness means not holding wrongs to their account or using their wrongs against them. For example, if I speak forgiveness toward a friend who has wronged me, and days later go and tell others about him, causing him to have a bad name, then I am holding it against them and charging the wrong to their account.

On the other hand, if I speak forgiveness toward that person, and do not mention what happened to anyone else, then I am carrying out the forgiveness that I have already spoken.

Have you ever tried to forget something? To most people, the more they try to forget, the more that situation comes to mind. I have a few childhood scares from various accidents. When I look at the scares, I can still remember how they came about. Even though my memory of the incident isn't gone, I noticed the pain has. It doesn't hurt like it did when it first happened.

This principle holds true with forgiveness. We may never forget, but the pain should grow weaker and weaker with time. We shouldn't feel guilty or think we haven't forgiven because we remember the incident. Instead, the real test of true forgiveness is whether we hold it against them.

Chapter Three Preview

Forgiveness: Why is it so hard?

A look at what's ahead:

- We fail to deal with the hurt.
- We misunderstand forgiveness.
- Forgiveness involves a long process.
- We see our sins as small compared to the sins of others.
- We have a lack of love for Christ.

Chapter 3

Forgiveness - Why Is It So Hard?

If we were to take a poll from all Christians with the question,

"What is the most difficult thing about being a Christian?"

I'm sure the most popular answer would be," forgiving others for the wrongs committed against us." One would think because we have the indwelling of the Holy Spirit, the inerrant Word of God, and the Blood of Jesus Christ shed on Calvary, that it would be easy as pie. But that's not the case at all. Here are some of the reasons our struggle with forgiveness is so severe.

We Fail to Deal With The Hurt

When they told Sophia about the accident, she felt in her heart that her three children were dead. Three years later, there was still a mountain of hurt associated with that tremendous tragedy. And now, on Mother's Day, the pain had become so intense that it seemed to be too much for her to handle.

As Sophia discovered, failing to deal with the hurt can cause a build-up of pain. Perhaps she needed to become involved in a grief support group. Perhaps she needed to talk with someone who was going through a similar situation. One thing for certain, like all of us, Sophia needed help to relieve the hurt. If not, she would be doomed to a life of heartache and pain.

We Misunderstand Forgiveness

Marvin sat in the grief support group with his mind elsewhere. Today was the fourth anniversary of the robbery and brutal murder of his loving wife of fourteen years.

"Group, I know it's a difficult thing to do, but today we are going to discuss how forgiveness plays a role in our grieving process," announced the grief counselor. Marvin stared at the counselor and muffled under his breath, "I'll die and go to Hell before I let that murderer off the hook!"

Hosea 4:6 says,

"My people are destroyed for lack of knowledge."

Surely what we don't know can cause us to remain in heartache and pain. Misunderstanding about forgiveness can leave us chained to anger and hatred for long periods of time. Marvin needed someone to explain that forgiveness doesn't let those who hurt us "off the hook." On the contrary, forgiveness doesn't free them. Rather, it frees us from a lifetime of bondage and hate.

Forgiveness Involves a Long Process

Steven couldn't understand why he continued to feel hatred toward his ex-wife. After all, it was years ago that she left him for another man while showering her lover with gifts funded from his bank account. Now, she professed to be a born-again believer in Christ, even apologizing several times to him for her past actions. Steven had followed the path of forgiveness, but wondered if he really had forgiven.

Steven discovered something that not many Christians are aware of: Forgiveness involves a long process. And for some people, it becomes a life-long process. In this microwave minded generation, It's not easy to become engaged in anything that's long and drawn out. Yes, Stephen had granted forgiveness to his ex-wife years ago, but he wasn't aware that it would take many more years to "work-out" the forgiveness he had spoken.

As an example, the Word of God states,

"Continue to work out your own salvation with fear and trembling."(Philippians 2:12)

Surely he doesn't mean we must continually work in order to achieve salvation. Salvation is a one-time act performed by God. It's not something that we must constantly strive for. I will put this scripture into contemporary terms:

"Now that you have been saved, start and continue to live your life in a way that reflects that salvation."

This also holds true in the arena of forgiveness. Once we have granted forgiveness as Jesus instructs us, then starts the long road of living in a manner that reflects forgiveness toward others. This road includes constant prayer and asking God to grant wisdom and a change of heart. It now becomes a process. And this process can be a very difficult road.

We See Our Sins as Small Compared to the Sins of Others.

When we think about the sins of others, we can easily become angry and frustrated. But when we think about our sins, we often be-little them and give excuses for our behavior. Jesus put it in these words,

"And why do you look at the speak in your brother's eye, but do not consider the plank in your own. Or how can you say to your brother, 'Let me remove the speak from your eye', and look, a plank is in your own eye?" (Matthew 7:3-4)

In these circumstances it becomes difficult to grant forgiveness while we have a "holier than thou" frame of mind toward the ones who hurt us. We must come to this accurate conclusion about ourselves:

"Just as the actions that others take against us hurt tremendously, so does our actions against God. Both my enemy and I are in need of Christ's forgiveness!"

We Have a Lack of Love for Christ.

Crystal stared at the Mother of the drunk driver who killed her daughter. As the judge pronounced the sentence, the Mother's anguish provided Crystal with a moment of satisfaction. Yes, Crystal knew Christ, but she wanted the Mother to feel the hurt and pain she had been carrying for several years. Crystal thought, "I want her to see how it feels to lose a child."

Christ speaks in John 14:21,

"He who has my commandments and keeps them, it is he who loves Me."

He is saying that our obedience is a result of our love for Him. In Crystal's case, her hatred and bitterness about the death of her daughter had overshadowed her love for Christ.

Instead of seeking to do the thing that pleased her Lord and Savior, she sought to fulfill her own desire for revenge. Simply put, willful disobedience results from a lack of love for Jesus.

Chapter Four Preview

Developing the Proper Motivation

A look at what's ahead:

- I forgive because it pleases God.
- I forgive because it shows love for others.
- I forgive because God will reward me

Chapter 4

Developing the Proper Motivation

Vera realized she had failed yet again. She knew she wasn't supposed to share Philip's name with others in a negative way. But here she was again, gathered with her sorority sisters, verbally beating up on Philip and scandalizing his name.

The breakup of their marriage five years ago wounded her deeply. They both decided to part as friends, but Vera continued to hold on to the hurt and bitterness through the years.

After their gathering, Vera went home and wept to the Lord, asking Him to, "Please help me to forgive Philip from my heart."

Vera had the right idea, but her results always seemed to fall short. She realized she wasn't making progress in her journey of forgiveness. She had often spoken the words of forgiveness but constantly failed in the area of working out that forgiveness.

By now, she should have mastered some of the disciplines like not intentionally making someone look bad, or speaking about them in a negative way before others. I wonder what was Vera's motivation.

Our motivation determines our outcome. It's not enough to know what to do. We must also have the proper motivation in order to succeed. Motivation can be defined as the driving force behind our actions. It's this driving force that will cause us to continue when we feel like giving up.

It's this driving force that will take us to success in spite of our sins and flaws. And it's this driving force that will ultimately see us to the finish line.

Let's take a lesson from the life of our Lord and Savior Jesus Christ. His first motivator was pleasing God. He says it in this manner,

"The Father has not left Me alone, for I always do those things that please him." John 8:29

It was this driving force that protected him from premature harm. It was this driving force that gave Him wisdom to respond to "trap questions." It was this driving force that strengthened and comforted Him in moments of intense anguish. And it was this driving force that led Him to Calvary's mountain to die for the sins of the world.

His second motivator was His love for us. Jesus speaks in John 10:10 and John 15:13,

"I have come that they may have life, and that they may have it more abundantly."

"Greater love has no one than this, than to lay down one's life for his friends."

It was this motivator that helped Jesus see the good in sinners when the religious community labeled them as outcasts. It was this motivator that allowed Him to love those who thought commandment keeping was a ticket to Heaven. And It was this motivator that led Him to forgive others even while they sought His life.

His third motivator was Himself. The Word of God reveals it in this manner,

"And being found in appearance as a man, He humbled Himself and became obedient to the point of death, even the death of the cross. Therefore, God has also

highly exalted Him and given Him the name which is above every name, that at the name of Jesus every knee should bow, of those in heaven, and of those on earth, and of those under the earth, and that every tongue should confess that Jesus Christ is Lord, to the glory of God the Father." (Phil 2:5-11)

Jesus knew His Father waited on the other side of the cross. And He knew about the glories, honor, authority, and exaltation He would receive from God the Father as a reward for doing God's will and loving others. He looked forward to rejoining the Father in paradise.

We can sum it all up in this simple acronym **JOY**: (Jesus, Others, Yourself).

What should your motivation be for forgiving?

1st : I forgive because I want to do what pleases God.

2nd : I forgive because it demonstrates love toward others.

3rd I forgive because the Lord will reward me (release from anger and bitterness).

Do you have a relationship with the Lord? Do you really desire to please Him? Can you see past that person's faults to see the need for Christ in their life? Do you really want to let go of all the anger, hurt, and bitterness in your life? Complete forgiveness will not be accomplished until your answer to all of these questions is "Yes".

Chapter Five Preview

Help Me Desire It! Taking a Closer Look

A look at what's ahead:

- Forgiveness reveals our love for God and others.
- Forgiveness reveals our mercy.
- Forgiveness reveals our hope.
- Forgiveness reveals our patience.
- Forgiveness reveals our humility.
- Forgiveness reveals our spiritual maturity.
- Forgiveness reveals our freedom
- Forgiveness reveals our obedience.

Chapter 5

Forgiveness: Help Me Desire It: Taking a Closer Look

Very few of us strive for something we don't want. In a previous chapter we talked about motivation. Now, we will combine motivation with our personal desires in order to create forgiveness in action.

Forgiveness is often portrayed by the Christian community as "something God expects us to do" or "something we must do in order to receive God's forgiveness." Both of these statements are true, however, forgiveness involves much more.

Let's take a closer look at forgiveness and point out some spiritual implications it brings into our lives.

Forgiveness reveals our love for God and others.

Forgiveness fulfills the greatest commandment,

"And you shall love the Lord your God with all your heart, with all your soul, with all your mind, and with all your strength.....You shall love your neighbor as yourself." (Mark 12:30-31)

When we grant forgiveness, we are putting love into action toward our Heavenly Father and toward those we forgive. This holds true in any relationship, whether it's between spouses, parent-child, or friend-to-friend, where there is true love, forgiveness will also be present.

Forgiveness revels our Mercy.

Time and time again we are instructed to walk in mercy toward others. Jesus constantly demonstrated mercy toward sinners while He walked on earth. We, being the children of God, are to follow His pattern of granting mercy. Mercy can be defined as not treating others according to what their sins deserve.

In my prayers, I constantly thank God with this statement, "I thank You for not treating me according to what my sins deserve. But instead, You have been kind, tenderhearted, and merciful." Just as God has mercy on us, so we must do likewise toward others.

Forgiveness revels our hope.

The scriptures constantly encourage us to never give up hope,

"And let us not grow weary while doing good, for in due season we shall reap if we do not lose heart." (Galatians 6:9)

When Jesus forgave Peter for denying Him, He showed that there was still hope for their relationship. When we forgive others, we model Jesus and send a strong message of hope that says,

"I can do all things through Christ who strengthens me." (Philippians 4:13)

Forgiveness reveals our Patience.

Patience is a fruit of the Spirit that all Christians should learn to cultivate. When we forgive, we are showing others that we are willing to give them another chance. In a parable told by Jesus, one man pleads with another,

"Have patience with me and I will pay you all. But he would not, but went and threw him into prison till he should pay the debt." (Matthew 18:29-30)

We must not have the thinking of Peter, who asked Jesus,

"Lord, how often shall my brother sin against me and I forgive him, up to seven times?"

Instead, we must have the thinking of Jesus when He responded,

"I do not say to you up to seven times, but up to seventy times seven." (Matthew 18:21-22)

Forgiveness reveals our Humility.

The Word of God cautions us not to think more highly of ourselves than we ought, and to consider others better than ourselves.

"For I say, through the grace given to me, to everyone who is among you, not to think of himself more highly than he ought to think.." (Romans 12:3)

"Let nothing be done through selfish ambition or conceit, but in lowliness of mind let each esteem others better than himself." (Philippians 2:3)

When we grant forgiveness, we are putting the virtue of humility into action and sending a resounding message to others that, "I am among you as one who serves."

Forgiveness reveals our Spiritual Maturity

Multiple times and in many various ways the scriptures admonish us to "grow up."

" For though by this time you ought to be teachers, you need someone to teach you again the first principles of the oracles of God; and you have come to need milk and not solid food. For everyone who partakes only of milk is unskilled in the word of righteousness, for he is a babe. But solid food belongs to those who are of full age, that is, those who by reason of use have had their senses exercised to discern both good and evil." (Heb 5:12-14)

We must grow from being babes in Christ to Christians who crave meat. When we forgive, spiritual maturity begins to take place and our growth in Christ is advancing.

While unforgiveness stunts our growth, forgiveness causes our growth to spring forward as we are being conformed into the image of our Lord and Savior.

Forgiveness reveals our Freedom.

Who desires to be chained and bound with anger and hatred? Through the sin of unforgiveness, we become prisoners to these horrible creatures as the scripture teaches,

"Most assuredly, I say to you, whoever commits sin, is a slave of sin." (John 8:34)

When we forgive we now have the freedom to live and walk in peace and joy. As it is written,

"Therefore, if the Son makes you free, you shall be free indeed." (John 8:36)

Forgiveness reveals our obedience.

Obedience is a sign of our love for Christ. When do as Christ says, and forgive, we are showing our love for Him. Jesus says it in this way,

"If you love me, keep my commandments." (John 14:15)

"He who has my commandments and keeps them, it is he who loves me." (John 14:21)

There is a reward and blessings connected with our obedience. When we forgive, regardless of how we feel, the words of God toward Jesus hold true for us,

"This is my beloved Son, in whom I am well pleased." (Matthew 3:17)

Chapter Six Preview

Walk Me Through It: Forgiveness From the Heart

A look at what's ahead:

- Speak forgiveness from the heart, not from emotions.
- Doing what is right often conflicts with what we feel.
- The two great laws at work in our lives.

Chapter 6

Walk Me Through It: Forgiveness From the Heart

Rhonda sat in the divorce hearing fighting back her tears. The hurtful lies and stories coming from her ex-husband were cutting her soul to pieces. How could someone who said they loved her try to ruin her life?

After all, she knew the truth. She was the one who tried everything she knew to keep the marriage together. She was the one who looked the other way after discovering his many affairs. She was the one who worked a second job to feed and cloth their three children after he was fired.

She was the one who tolerated being demeaned and abused for the past years. And after all of that, he had the nerve to slap her with a notice of divorce and engage in a battle to take the children away from her.

At the first break in the hearings, Rhonda's best friend escorted her out of the building and into the fresh air. "I know it really hurts you to hear all of those lies coming from someone you once loved, but I want you to forgive him for all the awful things he has done to you and your children." Her friend pleaded.

"No way!" Rhonda burst forth. "I want him to feel all the hurt I'm feeling! I want him to pay ten times over for destroying this family and trying to take my kids! There is no way I'm going to forgive him and let him off the hook!"

Rhonda's friend slowly pulled her close and warmly embraced her. "I didn't say that to let him off the hook. I said it so you can be let off the hook."

Rhonda stared at her, looking puzzled.

She consoled Rhonda. "Look at what the anger and bitterness is doing to you. It's destroying your whole life. You can't sleep at night, your health is failing, and your children notice the change in your behavior toward them."

She continued. "Forgiveness doesn't let him off the hook, but it does set you free. Please don't destroy yourself along with him You've got to learn to forgive."

As they embraced again Rhonda finally understood her situation. She knew her friend was correct. She needed relief from the inner wars and battles of bitterness and anger. Rhonda stared into her friend's eyes, "I need to forgive, but I don't know how. Please help me."

Rhonda's friend extended her hands, "Just repeat this prayer with me,

"Father, You know how much I've been hurt through all of this and You know the hurt of my children. Father, I'm asking you to forgive him, not because I want to, but because You said to forgive. I pray that You will remove all of this anger and hurt inside of me, and help me to love my enemies. I receive Your peace, comfort, and joy into my heart this very second. In Jesus name, Amen."

After the prayer Rhonda sensed the peace of God enter her. She seemed to have different facial expression during the next session: an expression of peace and contentment. She had found the secret to freeing herself from destruction through anger and bitterness. That secret was through forgiveness.

As Rhonda discovered, the first and most difficult step to take in forgiving others is bringing ourselves to speak the words from the heart (with the intent to live by them.)

It's very difficult to ask God to forgive those who hurt us, especially when the hurt has run deep. Our emotions are yelling, "Never!" But our spirit is whispering, "It's time to forgive, and move beyond this pain and anger."

We cannot afford to wait on our emotions to catch-up with what's right in our spirit. As a matter of fact, performing that which is spiritual often goes against what we are feeling; thus the two sides are often in conflict. To help us understand, let's examine the words found in Romans 7:21-23:

"So I find this law at work: When I want to do good, evil is right there with me. For in my inner being I delight in God's law; but I see another law at work in the members of my body, waging war against the law of my mind and making me a prisoner of the law of sin at work within my members."

These scriptures are talking about the two great laws at work in our lives; the law of righteousness, which knows and acknowledges the good things we should do, and the law of sin, which persuades us to do those things, which are wrong. In other words, spiritually, we know and want to do the right things, but in our bodies, we want to do the wrong thing.

How do we do the spiritual and right thing and yet at the same time satisfy our emotions? The answer is quite simple; it cannot be done. We must do that which is right and allow our emotions to complain in the process.

The way to do this to go to God in prayer and ask Him to forgive those who have wronged us, even if we are seeking forgiveness for ourselves. Remember, when we say the words, our emotions will not agree with them, but we will have accomplished something good and spiritual. In our emotions, we may still have the pain and anger, but our spirit will no longer be burdened by unforgiveness.

A suggested prayer may be:

"God, I'm asking You to forgive those who hurt me. In my heart I don't want to forgive, but I know this is what You want me to do, and I know it's the right thing to do. I ask In Jesus name. Amen."

Chapter Seven Preview

Walk Me Through It: God's Justice

A look at what's ahead:

- Ask God for justice, not revenge.
- Our justice is condemnation - punishment- destruction
- God's justice is conviction – discipline – restoration.
- A Christian has the right to ask God for justice.

Chapter 7

Walk Me Through It: God's Justice

Jake's stomach twisted in knots as he sat still in the courtroom listening to testimony about the murder. As his swollen and tear-soaked eyes moved slowly toward the accused murderer, he could envision the accused strapped in an electric chair with his own hands firmly on the power switch.

It was difficult for Jake to imagine how someone could take the life of his twelve-year-old daughter in such a cold and callous manner. He wanted with all his heart to take matters into his own hands. Instead, he momentarily pushed aside the anger, buried his face in his hands, and wept bitterly.

As the prosecutor continued questioning the accused murderer, each gruesome detail of his daughter's murder seemed to push him further to the breaking point. "I wish I could just get my hands around his throat just for one minute." Jake thought. Just then, the warm hands of his brother touched his shoulders in a gesture of support.

During the break in proceedings, Jake's brother expressed his concern. "Jake, I can't begin to imagine what you are going through right now. It must be nothing short of Hell itself. But I'm very concerned about you and the family."

"Don't be," Jake quickly answered. "We'll be a lot better after they fry this thing who calls himself a man!" I want to have the front row seat that's close enough to see every wrinkle of pain on his face!"

Jake's brother took a deep breath. "We all want justice for want happened. It was a terrible thing. But justice is what we should all ask God for, and not revenge." He explained.

"What are you talking about?" Jake screamed. "Are you telling me I'm wrong to want to see him squirm in pain for killing my little girl?"

"Jake, it's only natural to want to hurt somebody who has caused you so much pain." Jake's brother confided. "But I'm cautioning you not to get your mind set on his punishment being a death sentence. I'm asking you to ask God for justice, knowing that He can touch the hearts of the judge and jury. But you must be willing to accept the punishment God allows."

"I can't do that!" Jake exclaimed. "I want to see him get what he deserves, even if I have to give it to him myself!"

Jake's brother softly touched him on the shoulder, "Can I at least pray for you?" Jake nodded his head in agreement. He prayed,

"Lord, we ask for justice. We are leaving his punishment up to you, to do whatever You see fit. We totally give him over into your hands. I also ask You to remove the anger and bitterness my brother carrying. I ask in Jesus' name. Amen"

Jake discovered there are incidents in life that hurt us in such a tremendous manner, that forgiveness seems to be impossible. As in Jake's case, the pain of losing his daughter to a cold-blooded killer seems to have ended his life as well. In his case, he has a long road to travel in order to achieve the forgiveness that God wants him to extend, but the road must begin with justice, not revenge.

Justice is turning someone over to the proper authorities, to deal with them according to the established laws of the land. In contrast, revenge is our attempt to take the law into our own hands and issue the punishment we think is best.

When we ask God for justice, we are turning our case over to the proper authority, which is God. We are asking God to do that which He knows is best. All sin is punished. Therefore, they will not get off scott-free. God will issue the punishment that best fits the crime. We want to see them get what they deserve, and to us, they deserve the harshest of treatment. What we are expecting and what God wants are two different things.

Our brand of justice is condemnation, punishment, and destruction. However, God's brand of justice is conviction, discipline, and then restoration.

Some Christians may not think its right to ask for justice. It's not only proper to do, it's our God given right as His children. To illustrate this point, there is a story in the Bible about a persistent widow who had been wronged (Luke 18:1-8). The widow urged the judge to grant her justice against her adversary. Eventually, the judge fulfilled the plea of the widow.

Jesus' point in this parable was simply this: If she could get justice from an ungodly man, surely we can get justice from God! If we ask God for that which is right in His sight, we can trust Him to deliver!

Chapter Eight Preview

Walk Me Through It: Dealing with the Anger

A look at what's ahead:

- Ask God to remove the anger.
- Hurt and anger lying dormant will resurface.
- We must seek God in an honest attempt to be healed.

Chapter 8

Walk Me Through It: Dealing With the Anger

Jodie tried with all she had to fit in with the discussion group, but something within her wouldn't allow it. She thought, "I don't belong here. All of these people are filled with so much anger and bitterness. Is this a picture of me in the upcoming years?"

"Group, we have a new member tonight and her name is Jodie," the counselor for the Christian rape recovery group announced. "Jodie, would you like to share some thoughts with the group?" Jodie thought for a moment. It surprised her that the first thoughts she wanted to share were those of anger and hatred for her convicted rapist. It happened over three years ago, but the deep emotional wounds were still fresh.

As she began to speak, tears welled up in her eyes and a knot formed in her stomach. She hung her head and motioned to the counselor to continue with the discussion without her.

After the meeting, the counselor took her to a private room and began to share some things with her. "Jodie, I've seen many hurt, angry, and confused women come through this group. I want to share something with you.

The women who successfully make it to full recovery all share one thing in common: They confessed their hurt. Have you talked to someone about how the rape made you feel?"

Jodie wiped her tears, "No, not really. I just can't seem to talk about it right now."

The counselor peered into her eyes and whispered, "I understand if you are not ready now, but eventually the hurt must be confessed in some form. Perhaps it would help if you wrote it down or even better if you acknowledged it to God in your prayers."

"But God already knows how I feel." Jodie responded.

"Yes He does. But He still wants you to confess your hurt to Him so healing can begin. The Counselor interjected. "He can't heal what we don't confess." As the counselor gently pulled her head to her shoulders, she asked Jodie, "Can I lead you in prayer?"

"Yes." Jodie sobbed. The counselor prayed:

"Father God, I realize You know my hurt and anger, but I want to share it with You anyway. When this happened to me, I felt violated, used, and totally shameful. I cried out for help, but no one came. I'm filled with anger, confusion, bitterness, and shame. Father, I need You to help me through this. I'm asking you to remove my bitterness, and restore the joy to my life. In Jesus name, Amen."

After the prayer Jodie could feel an enormous weight lifted from her shoulders. She experienced the peace that only God brings as a result of confession.

Jodie discovered that hurt and anger lying dormant will soon resurface. We discussed earlier in this book about the danger of remaining in anger. Now we need to seek a way out and a release from the bondage of anger. When we think about that life-changing event, anger begins to rise within our emotions. We may have a right to be angry, but not a right to remain in anger.

Understandably, we've been hurt, but when we seek God and make an honest attempt to be healed, He will bring us into a higher level of understanding. Little by little, He will reveal things that will help us let go of the hurtful anger. I call this "transformation of the mind". God will help us see the situation in a different way, and even lead us into a different view of our adversary. Instead of looking upon ourselves with pity, God will teach us to look upon our adversary with pity.

As God transforms our thinking, He also removes the anger while replacing it with wisdom, mercy, and peace. Continue to seek God in every way possible and He will loosen the hold of anger. A suggested prayer is:

"God, You know my emotions. I'm asking You to remove the anger within me and teach me to be merciful, wise, and strong, in Jesus name, Amen."

Chapter Nine Preview

Walk Me Through It: Receiving God's Peace

A look at what's ahead:

- Ask God to dull the pain and grant peace.
- Three great areas of peace.
- Peace with God.
- Peace with others.
- Peace within.

Chapter 9

Walk Me Through It: Receiving God's Peace

Now that we have addressed the anger, we can finally deal with the painful moment. Its quite natural to hurt in hurtful situations. We shouldn't expect all of the pain to completely disappear, or our memory to go blank. However, God can bring us to a point of "dulled pain" and instill His peace in our hearts, which leads to a joyful life.

We may think, "I'll never have joy in my life again." We may have lived so long in anger and bitterness that the experience of joy may have been forgotten.

For some of us we merely need to laugh, be carefree, enjoy the sunshine, and bask in the beauty that God has provided on earth. It's been far too long since we've smiled a genuine smile or laughed a genuine laugh. For some of us, these things are long overdue.

This is an area where we can actually help ourselves. We must learn to speak positive things about the situation. We may not be able to speak positively about the incident itself, but we can speak positively about the circumstances. We can say things like, "I know God is giving me peace. I know the pain is being dulled and the joy is returning."

When we speak positively instead of waiting on a feeling to come, we begin to determine our own outcome. If we continue to speak negative words we are setting the stage for a negative outcome. If we continue in the positive, in time, the peace of God will come into our lives and the joy of the Lord will manifest itself.

Every so often we will feel the dulled pain, but the joy and peace of God will rule in our lives.

A suggested prayer is:

"Lord, You know how much I'm hurting. I ask You to dull the pain, increase Your peace, and restore the joy in my life, in Jesus name, Amen."

Chapter Ten Preview

Walk Me Through It: Learning to Trust God

A look at what's ahead:

- Trust God.
- God loves us.
- God is aware of our situation.
- God is in control.

Chapter 10

Walk Me Through It: Learning to Trust God

Proverbs 3:5-6 says:

"Trust in the Lord with all your heart and lean not on your own understanding; in all your ways acknowledge Him, and He will make your paths straight."

To trust God sounds simple and straight to the point. But it's not as easy as it sounds. Trust means to believe even though we don't fully understand. It's easy to trust when we understand, but difficult to do when we don't understand. We must believe God is at work even when things don't seem to be going our way.

We must trust Him when the human justice system fails, when we witness the callous and prideful behavior of the adversary, when it seems as if the guilty will go unpunished, and trust Him regardless of what the circumstances may seem.

A songwriter penned these words, "God is working, even in the rain." This means God is doing His will and bringing about His purpose, even in our rainy or bad situations.

We mentioned, earlier, the author of Psalms 73. He looked on the wicked and thought God wasn't doing anything about them. We too will eventually come into an understanding about God. He works not on our time frame, but on His. He works not by our judgments, but by His. Once we grasp and retain this spiritual truth, trusting Him will become easier.

A suggested prayer is:

"Lord, teach me to trust You. Teach me not to abandon You when things don't turn out my way. I know you are a God of Your word, in Jesus name, Amen"

Chapter Eleven Preview

Self Forgiveness: How do I forgive Myself?

A look at what's ahead:

- Receiving God's forgiveness means receiving our forgiveness.
- We are not God. We must allow ourselves room to be human.
- God knows about our sins beforehand, yet he still chose us.
- We are not what we have done.

Chapter 11

Self Forgiveness: How Do I forgive Myself?

It was extremely noisy in the day care center. The children were running to and fro, scampering around like little chicks chasing a worm. As Trina sat in the lobby, waiting for the instructor to bring her 3 year-old daughter, suddenly another anxiety attack struck. It was triggered by the voices of the children. It hadn't happened in quite some time, but suddenly she heard the cries of infant babies ringing in her ears.

Her hands began to sweat as she sprang to her feet, covered her mouth with her hands, and ran out of the center into the fresh air. As she stood close to the road, gasping for air, the thoughts of the horror of four years ago returned.

Trina had forgiven her mother and her boyfriend for persuading her to have an abortion, but the person she found the most difficult to forgive was herself.

She had taken her feelings of condemnation to God time and time again but always seemed to leave with them on her shoulders. After the attacks became more frequent, she finally confided in her Pastor. Her Pastor spoke these words:

"Trina, we all make mistakes in this life and some of our mistakes tend to haunt us unless we learn a few key things:

1. ***We are not God.*** We are humans. And as humans we are subject to make the wrong choices and decisions. We cannot see as God sees and know as He does.

2. ***God knows about our sins*** and mistakes before we commit them. However, He still chose to love and accept us in spite of them.

3. **We are not what we have done.** God can see us without holding our sins over our heads. He forgave us BEFORE we made the mistake and have forgiven us for our future mistakes.

4. **Your child is not lost.** Your child is with God. And when you see your child again, you won't have to explain what happened on earth, all you will need to do is love that child for eternity!"

Trina could sense that load of guilt and condemnation melt away from her as they prayed. God's peace had truly set her free from the condemnation of sin.

To receive God's forgiveness is to forgive ourselves. Once we come to the altar, we can pray:

"Father in heaven, I come to you rejoicing because You have known my mistakes beforehand. You have wiped my sins away through the blood of Jesus. I am free from sin and guilt and alive to Your mercy and grace. I thank You for choosing me in spite of my flaws, and I thank you for preserving my child until we meet in eternity. I receive Your peace in my heart at this very moment. In the name of Jesus Christ. Amen"

Chapter Twelve Preview

The Healing Starts With You!

A look at what's ahead:

- Christ sets us free for reasons that go beyond ourselves.
- Hurting people hurt other people.
- Our obedience can cause others to be set free.

Chapter 12

The Healing Starts With You.

"bearing with one another, and forgiving one another, if anyone has a complaint against another; even as Christ forgave you, so you also must do." (Col 3:13)

Jeneva rang the doorbell to her father's house, but she didn't want to. As she stood on the porch nervously waiting for the elderly man to answer the door, her mind faded back to those moments of abuse he inflicted on her as a child.

Those wounds of abuse had managed to destroy her twelve-year marriage and separate her from her children. Now, two years after a divorce and release from a mental institution, Jeneva was finally preparing to confront the man whom she often said, "Destroyed my life."

But during the past two years, Jeneva managed to find Christ in an intimate way. It was because of His healing, comforting, and strengthening that she was able to bring herself to her father's doorstep. She had laid her wounds at the feet of Jesus and received His perfect peace. Now, she was being led by the Holy Spirit to confront her abuser and she didn't have a clue what she would say or do.

As she prayerfully waited, the door slowly opened. She gazed upon the face of her father for the first time in over ten years. "Hi." Jeneva said, as she forced a smile on her face. She could see from his appearance that the years had taken their toll on him.

He seemed very surprised to see her and after a moment of staring, managed to muffle, "It's been a long time. I thought you forgot about me after your Mother died."

Jeneva felt very awkward and he finally motioned for her to come in. As they took their seats, the conversation turned to the usual small talk. After Jeneva updated him on her failed marriage and family, he didn't seem to take much interest. In fact, he didn't seem surprised at all by the outcome of her life.

During a moment of silence the Holy Spirit whispered to Jeneva, "Tell him you're sorry and ask him to forgive you."

What! Jeneva thought. Why should I do that? He was the one who abused me! After wrestling with the thought for several minutes she finally set her mind to do it.

Jeneva rose from her seat, "Well, I've got to go now so maybe I will stop by some other time." She took a deep breath, walked toward him, knelt down in front of him, and took him by the hand.

"Dad, I know our relationship hasn't been like a real father and daughter and I want you to know that I am sorry for not being there for you after mom passed away. I know I've never said this before, but I love you and I want you to love me too. Please forgive me." Jeneva gave him a warm hug.

As they embraced, her father could sense something wonderfully different about his daughter. Never before had they embraced like father and daughter should. At that moment he felt the conviction of all the years of abuse he inflicted and began to burst into tears.

"What's wrong?" Jeneva asked.

All he could say was, "I'm sorry sweetheart....I'm sorry..."

For the first time he began to share the abuse from his childhood. As he spoke of those awful moments, Jeneva held him tightly, and they both continued to shed tears.

It was then that the Holy Spirit helped Jeneva to understand something significant: Hurting people hurt others. Now she understood why the Holy Spirit led her to begin the healing. As they continued to embrace and cry together, the Holy Spirit was at work, healing them both from years of hatred and abuse.

Forgiveness

Can you identify with Jeneva? Is the Holy Spirit leading you to begin the healing? If so, follow His lead.

Chapter Thirteen Preview

Forgiveness: The Need for God.

A look at what's ahead:

- True Forgiveness cannot be accomplished without God.
- He gives us knowledge, peace, joy, and hope.
- God is very real and very understandable.

Chapter 13

The Need for God

True forgiveness cannot be achieved without having God in our lives. It is God who provides all the necessary components to over-come the negatives of unforgiveness. He provides us with the knowledge that will lead us into a higher level of thinking. He provides us with the peace that helps us to stand in the midst of those trying times.

He gives us the true joy that we experience in those days and hours that we feel like throwing in the towel. He calms and cools our anger when we seem to go beyond the point of no return. And finally, God gives us that one ray of hope when all else seems hopeless.

I know from experience. If it were not for having a personal relationship with God through Jesus Christ, I would certainly be a total basket case from the wounds and disappointments of my life. I'm not talking about becoming "religious" or joining a denomination. I'm talking about forming a real relationship with a person who loves and cares for me.

Through this relationship He makes His presence known in multiple ways, and His presence revolves around my needs. When I'm feeling lonely or like no one really cares, He comes and makes His presence known by giving me comfort. Some people call it a warm fuzzy feeling that everything is going to be all right.

When I'm feeling over-come with anger or anxiety, He comes to me and brings His peace. When I need someone to have a conversation with, He is there waiting to listen and speak words of encouragement into my heart.

God is a personal God. He forms relationships and has expectations for all those who receive Him. He is not some mystical figment of someone's imagination. He is very real and very understandable. But most of all, He is the only person who understands me better than I understand myself. He knows my wants, needs, shortcomings, and desires. Still, even after all my shortcomings; He wants to form a solid relationship with me in order to help me through the tough times of my life.

God wants to help anyone who receives Him and acknowledges Jesus Christ as their Lord and Savior. With God you don't have to go through a background check, application, aptitude test, and no witnesses or references are needed. He only asks you to believe in Him and give Him a try. A suggested prayer is:

"God, I need someone to help me through these hard times. I believe You can and will. I believe Jesus died and lived again in order to help me live a victorious life. I confess Jesus as my Lord and Savior and give my life totally to You. In Jesus name, Amen."

Chapter Fourteen Preview

Forgiveness: It's Not About You!

A look at what's ahead:

- Clarissa's story
- Our wounds happened to us, but they are not about us.
- My personal testimony.
- What you've gone through is not about you; it's all about God!

Chapter 14

It's Not About You

Clarissa sat silently in the huge auditorium two hours before she was to speak to a crowd of about six thousand people. As she meditated on the words to be delivered from the scriptures, suddenly and softly, a voice spoke to her,

"Clarissa, it's not about you….its all about Me."

It was then that Clarissa understood why God allowed all those horrible things to invade her life. The crowds of people she encouraged, inspired, and led to the Lord were the fruit of many years of heartache and pain.

She had always thought the incest and rape was all about her. She was convinced the breast cancer was strictly about her. And certainly, losing the fairy-tail husband to a younger woman was totally about her. Now, she saw and understood things from a different point of view. She saw things through the eyes of God.

She also saw the scriptures from a different perspective. When she re-read the story about the man born blind, she could actually see herself in the man. Her only question was, "Lord, how could You allow this man to be born blind, to suffer for so long, just to reveal your glory?" As she continued to meditate, the answer came to her,

"He has been given a passion to testify to My name, and He has received much more reward than you can ever imagine."

I think we all can identify with Clarissa to some respect. We often think the unfortunates in our lives are all about us.

"Why did this have to happen to ME?"

"What am I going to do now?"

"I am so hurt by all of this!"

"How do You expect Me to continue to live after this?"

These are just a few of the questions and statements that reveal a self-centered theology about our troubles and trials. We become so focused on ourselves, that we miss the ultimate opportunity to reveal God to a dying and disappointing world.

There are opportunities to witness for God in suffering, in pain, in heartaches, in injustice, and even in death. We all have "platform moments" in our lives. I refer to them as platform moments because of what is written in the Word of God.

In 1 Corinthians 4:9 Paul writes about the worldly injustice the Apostles were suffering. God had allowed his servants to be placed on a platform of suffering. Why? So the world could get a glimpse of God's glory!

I've been there…done that…got the tee-shirt! I know what its like to be on that platform.

On October 19th, 2001, our thirteen year old suddenly collapsed from a heart attack and died within minutes. A few days afterward, during his funeral, I was preparing to deliver the Eulogy. As I sat there, between my weeping wife and somber little daughter, fixing my eyes on his casket a few feet away from us, I suddenly discovered the pain was much too great for me to bare.

Forgiveness

After asking God for the peace that passes understanding, I slowly stepped up to the pulpit. There was a moment of complete silence that seemed to last for hours. There were many people in the audience who were wondering about my walk with the Lord.

"I wonder if He really knows Christ."

"Is this Christian thing real?"

"Will he give God glory, or will he breakdown in tears?"

I took a deep breath, glanced at our son's body a few feet away from me, and began to speak,

"You're probably wondering, why isn't he crying? I want you to know today that I've spent some time down in the valley. I've stumbled around in the darkness. I've had my moments when I've felt as weak as water. And I've cried till I have run out of tears.

But I also want you to know today, that my God has come. And He has strengthened me. He's picked my feet up out of the valley and placed them on the mountain top."

With those words being said, the people in that little church burst forth into praise. Some began to weep and shed tears. They realized that we were in the midst of the most hurtful moments of our lives, but God was with us! It wasn't about us, it was about Him!

I didn't realize it at the time, but God placed us on a platform. Thank God we used the platform to give Him glory! Even in one of the darkest times of our lives, we gave Him Glory!

If you think for one New York minute that all the hurtful occurrences in your life are all about you...then you are dead wrong! They are but platforms and spotlights yielding opportunities to show the world how good, faithful, and loving God is, even in the pain!

You may be on your platform as you read this book. If so, I'll give you a little wisdom.

What you're going through is not about you…Its all about God Yes it's happening to you, but it's not about you. It's all about Him. So tell someone about His goodness, His mercy, and His love. Use your platform to His glory.

Prayer: My great and loving Father. I don't understand the things I need to, but I know in spite of the things that have happened to me, that You love me. Help me to see my situation through Your eyes and Your mind. Help me to give You glory and praise in spite of. Help my lips to sing of Your love forever. In the name of Jesus Christ. Amen.

Now let's begin our journey of forgiveness. Remember, it all starts with you!

Forgiveness Journal:

People I need to Forgive:
_____

_____

_____

_____

_____

Reasons I need to Forgive:
_____

_____

_____

_____

_____

Date I asked God to Forgive Them (or Myself):
_____

_____

_____

Date I was able to release the anger and hurt:

_____

_____

_____

_____

My feelings toward them began to change on this date:

_____

_____

_____

_____

Date God gave me peace:

_____

_____

_____

_____

_____

Other Notes:

Charlie L. & Cassandra L Holley

Charlie & Cassandra are residents of Madison Alabama and founders of CL Holley Ministries, Inc., a ministry of comfort, encouragement, and inspiration. In 2001, their thirteen-year-old son suddenly and tragically died from cardiac arrest while playing basketball.

After going through deep dark depression, despair, and hopelessness, they both found Jesus Christ in a personal way.

Now, they travel to churches, schools, grief groups, and other organizations, carrying a message of hope and inspiration.

Visit them on their website for the latest in ministry events, to request speaking engagements, or to purchase books.

Website: www.clhmin.org   email: clholley@yahoo.com

Other Books by CL Holley:

The Power of Christian Comfort

The God of My Midnights
Finding Him in Our Darkest Moments

Lord, Fix My Leaks!
Comfort, Guidance, and Counsel for the Daughters of God
(An inspiring and empowering book for women)

Inspirations from the Scriptures
(A devotional filled with wisdom and encouragement)

Visit CharlieHolleyMinistries.org for more info.

Made in the USA
Charleston, SC
01 September 2015